The Improvement of the Moral Qualities

Philosopher Rabbi

Solomon Ibn Gabirol

SimchatChaim.com

There is no known book without mistakes. Therefore, I ask in every language of application if anyone has any questions, comments, clarifications, corrections, please send to: simchatchaim@yahoo.com

All material used in this section may not be used for commercial purposes, but only for study and teaching.

To get this book or books and information Email me at:

TABLE OF CONTENTS

Rabbi Solomon Ibn Gabirel

This great Hebrew poet and philosopher was born in Malaga, Spain, about the year 4782, (1021), and died in Valencia, Spain, at the age of 36 or 37.

Despite his very short life, Rabbi Solomon ibn Gabirel won great fame during his own lifetime, and even more so after his death when his writings became more widely known.

His father Yehuda, was a native of the famous city of Cordova which was at the time under Arab domination. About ten years before Solomon's birth, when war broke out in that part of the Spanish peninsula, his father moved to Saragossa, also under Arab domination. Later they moved to Malaga, where Rabbi Solomon was born.

Losing his parents at an early age, Rabbi Solomon nevertheless continued his studies of the Talmud, in which he found his only solace. The young Rabbi Solomon was an ardent scholar and became very proficient in the Hebrew as well as Arabic languages and grammar. He also studied astronomy, geometry, and philosophy:

Rabbi Solomon Ibn Gabirel began writing Hebrew poetry when he was very young. At the age of 16 he wrote a famous poem beginning with the words, "I am the master, and Song is my slave." This poem entitled "Azharoth," is based on the Taryag (613) commandments of the Torah, and was included in the Shavuoth service of many congregations.

In that year, the famous Rav Hal Gaon died in Babylon, and Solomon ibn Gabirel wrote four dirges (obituary poems) on the passing of this great scholar.

Rabbi Solomon Ibn Gabirel sang the praises of Rabbi Samuel Hanagid and also of another Jewish minister, Jekuthiel ibn Hasan of Saragossa. The latter became Rabbi Solomon Ibn Gabirel's friend and patron. Unfortunately, Rabbi Ibn Hasan met with a violent death through a false accusation by his enemies. Rabbi Solomon Ibn Gabirel, who was about eighteen or nineteen years old at that time, composed a touching eulogy on the loss of his friend.

A number of Rabbi Solomon Ibn Gabirel's religious hymns were included in the prayer book. These include in addition to "Azharoth" mentioned above, his "Shir Hakovod" (Song of Glory), and "Shir Hayichud" (Song of Unity). Another of his famous poems is "Kether Malchuth" (Royal Crown). Rabbi Solomon Ibn Gabirel also wrote "Kinoth" (dirges) on the destruction of the Temple and the plight of Israel. His most famous book he wrote was **The Improvement of the Moral Qualities**. This books discusses Jewish philosophy of the soul and it relations to the four elements of the world.

Rabbi Solomon Ibn Gabirel's life was not a very happy one, for he was a lonesome young man with a sensitive soul. He did not hesitate to use his poetic gifts in denouncing the lack of Jewish feeling on the part of some prominent members of his community. As a result of this, he acquired many enemies who made life in Saragossa miserable for him. Eventually, Rabbi Solomon Ibn Gabirel was banished from his native town and spent some years as a luckless wanderer, suffering many hardships. No wonder there is a touch of bitterness in his poems, but this is often coupled with a sense of humor.

At the age of only 23, Rabbi Solomon Ibn Gabirel wrote his book "Tikkun Middoth Hanefesh," (Improvement of the Qualities of the Soul). About the same time he also wrote "Mivchar Hapeninim," (Choice of Pearls). Both were written in Arabic and subsequently translated into Hebrew by Rabbi Yehuda ibn Tibbon. In these books, Rabbi Solomon Ibn Gabirel presents a collection of moral sayings and maxims from Jewish as well as non-Jewish sources.

The manner of Rabbi Solomon Ibn Gabirel's death is shrouded in mystery. Legend has it that he was trampled to death by an Arab horseman, much in the same way that Rabbi Yehuda Halevi lost his life.

Introductory Essay

TRANSLATION OF THE IMPROVEMENT OF THE MORAL QUALITIES

This is an essay on the improvement of the moral qualities (i.e., character), according to the opinion of the greatest of the ancient sages, composed by the learned, the worthy, the scholarly Solomon ben Gabirel, the Israelite, the philosopher may God sanctify his soul. He composed it in the city of Saragossa, in the month of Nissan, in the year 828 of the Alexandrian era.

Blessed be God, the Mighty, the Wise, the One who is nigh, Responsive, the One, the Eternal, the Primordial, the Creator; greatly exalted be He. Verily, when we look at man who is the best of all the creatures of the Creator, exalted be His majesty, we recognize that he is the object aimed at in the creation of all substances and beings. Furthermore, he is best proportioned, as regards constitution, of all living beings; and, in addition to this, most perfect and most beautiful of form, and most completely fashioned. He possesses a rational soul, elemental, wise, everlasting, which does not perish with him. For all this there are clear proofs, both intellectual and Scriptural, which every intelligent man knows. The surest proof that man is pre-eminent among creatures is, that he partakes of the state of the angels in regard to speech and understanding. These two are divine and spiritual properties. Nay more, we see, besides this, that the angels busy themselves with the righteous man, as we learn from the case of Abraham, peace be unto him, in that they brought him glad tidings and also warned him; likewise from the case of Isaac and Jacob, our fathers. The latter said in the course of his excellent prayer for his son, "The angel which redeemed me"; and Scripture says of him, "Yea, he had power over the angel and prevailed"; and Daniel said, "My God hath sent his angel." Concerning the help vouchsafed to the pious and the destruction of their enemies, it is said, "And it came to pass that night that the angel of the Lord went out and smote in the camp of the Assyrians." There are many similar examples, which I will not go to the length of enumerating.

We know that some men may undoubtedly be superior to others, nay more, that one man may be equal to a large number of men although they be of one form and one composition, except that the soul of one man is predisposed to worldly honor, with the help of the celestial bodies, and his preference for ethical practice, and because the baser part of him is obedient to the higher, i.e., his intellect exercises control over his physical nature. But if his aim be low and his station unfit to reach that distinction, so that he does not rise to that control of which the bodies in their course have not given promise, i.e., a sign, or to which ethics have not aided him.

Then the wise and intelligent man ought to expend all his efforts in order to reach the highest dignity which he seeks, in order that it may be, as one of the sages said, "Help the celestial bodies with your souls, even as tilling and irrigating help the seed to grow"; and this occurs naturally through the instrumentality of the earth. He should endeavor to be one of the number of the excellent and through his zeal follow in their steps. Further, he must refine his qualities until they be improved and not employ his senses except when it appears necessary, until he becomes one (of those) who is honorably known and famed for his excellence, for that is worldly happiness. But when man reaches it, his eyes must not cease to gaze wistfully at the attainment of that which is above it, i.e., enduring happiness which he can reach in the intellectual world, the world to come. For this is the highest gift of God to His servants, in addition to the favor which is their common lot as existent creatures. The prince David, peace be unto him, had implored that he might attain to the well-being of this world, in saying, "Make with me a covenant for goodness." He also desired to be one of those well fitted to attain the bliss of the world to come, in that he said, "O how great is the goodness which Thou hast laid up for them that fear Thee". "They shall be abundantly satisfied with the fatness of Thy house." This height cannot be reached by any one save through merit. Thus he asked: "Lord, who shall abide in thy tabernacle, who shall dwell in thy holy hill?" And the answer is, "He that walketh uprightly and worketh righteousness." Having arrived in the course of our remarks at this stage in the account of man's pre-eminence, let us direct our attention to the statement of the object of this our work and the method of deriving some advantage therefrom. This will come to pass after we shall have divided the treatise into all its sections as is incumbent upon us. Then will we realize the benefit of it. Thus Solomon the Wise, peace be unto him, has said, "Behold this have I found, saith the Preacher, counting one by one to find out the account"; by which he meant to say that when things are brought together, it is necessary to enumerate them. So, also, by properly ordering the discourse, it will be understood.

God, Mighty and Exalted, has created the expanse of the smaller world, dependent upon four elements: He places in man blood corresponding to air, yellow gall corresponding to fire, black gall corresponding to earth, and white moisture corresponding to water. Moreover God, exalted be He, equipped him, i.e., man, with perfectness of form and with every organ complete and not wanting in any respect; and He created within him five senses, as we shall relate. Solomon the Wise alludes to them when he says, "I returned and saw under the sun"; "seeing" here means to observe carefully, the general term for "seeing" being here used in the place of the specific term, "observing carefully" as in saying, "under the sun," he means whatever the sun encircles.

In the saying, "The race is not to the swift," he hints at the sense of smell, which is (situated in) the nose, because running is impossible except through the inhalation of air from without to cool the natural heat which is within man. The inhalation is accomplished by the sense of the nose, and if there were no nose there could be no breathing, which causes motion.

In saying "Nor is the battle to the strong," he wishes to indicate the sense of hearing; just as we see that war consists of crying and of hearing in battle, as it is said "There is a noise of war in the camp."

In saying, "Nor yet is bread to the wise," he refers to the sense of taste and the meaning is to be taken literally.

In saying "Nor yet riches to the understanding," he refers to the sense of touch, which is of a kind with the understanding: that Gabirel follows Aristotle in bringing the sense of touch into relation with the understanding; The latter is of the category of the inner senses, which are concealed in the nature of the soul, as for example, perception, thought, and understanding.

In saying, "Nor is there favor to men of skill," he wishes to indicate the sense of sight, which does not become knowledge except through prolonged attention to scripture and continuous study of books. Were it not for the great length involved and our love of conciseness, we would follow up these allusions with clear arguments, (adduced) from syllogistic reasoning and the science of oral traditions, in order that they might be easily and simply comprehended. But for those whose faculties are above the ordinary and who are of high-minded purpose, this little will suffice as evidence that the wise prince alluded to naught else in this passage but the visible (outer) senses, and veiled the mention of the hidden (inner) ones.

If a man be wise, he will employ them in the right place and restrain them from everything in connection with which he ought not to use them. Let him rather be like a skillful physician, who prepares prescriptions, taking of every medicine a definite quantity; thus the ingredients vary in quantity; he uses of one the weight of a Danik, and of the other the weight of a Kirat; and so on according to his estimate of their respective effects. He will not be satisfied until there be mixed in with it something which will keep it from doing harm (to the person to whom it is administered), and all this must be calculated.

Since this is so, man ought to consider carefully the qualities which belong to his senses and not employ them except when it is necessary; for God, exalted be He, has so constituted them in man that he can wisely order them, since through them he guards the normal condition of his life. By their means he sees colors, hears sounds, tastes food (flavors), smells odors, distinguishes between hard and soft, and all other things which are necessary to his life; and many which are useful we will mention when we commence (the subject), please God. We will now describe the senses and the various advantages to be derived from their use and the necessity of refraining from the use of them when they would cause harm.

We hold that the first and foremost of the senses is that of the eye, since its position with regard to the body is like that of the sun to the universe. It is a sense which never fails to perceive an object without (the lapse of) time, specifically its perception of that which is near to it is as quick as its perception of that which is far from it; nor does any time elapse between its perception of the near and its perception of the far, as is the case with the other senses. The eye alights upon its objects of perception as long as it is open. Therefore, sleep is impossible unless it be closed. How wondrous is the saying of a philosopher with regard to the sense of the eye!" The soul has spiritual tints, which sometimes become apparent in the motion of the eyelid." Again he said, "Keep watch over the sense of sight: verily it may lead to various kinds of wrong: by some of its motions it may testify to your (having) pride and haughtiness, and by others to your possession of meekness and humility. Therefore, compel it to make the very best movements and restrain it from the most ignoble." "Furthermore," he said, "social intercourse does not exist for the pleasure of the eye, but the enjoyment of the mind." The learned man will understand this saying. How beautiful is the agreement of this utterance with the word of God, exalted and magnified be He, "Do ye not seek after your own heart and your own eyes."

The sense of hearing is next in point of importance. Though the effect of this sense upon the soul is more readily felt than that of sight, man does not heed it as he does the eye. Under good training, with reference to this sense, is included man's refraining from listening to indecent things, and not judging in regard to the pleasant tones which he hears according to their sound, but according to their meaning and intent. One ought not to be ensnared by what he hears, as the bird is ensnared by the sounds to which it inclines with admiration; and one ought to know of the places where it is necessary to pay good heed and those wherein it is not fitting to listen at all, as he of whom it is said, "that stoppeth his ears from the hearing of blood."

The sense of smell follows the sense of hearing, because a sound is felt in the air; and it is of lesser moment than the sense of hearing. Accordingly, there is less need of training it, because it entails not (the possibility of) obedience or revolt. As for taste, though it be, in degree, below the senses aforementioned, still the manner of training it is more important, for the body cannot exist without it, as it can exist without the others. The way to train it is, keep it from that which is forbidden, and give it free rein with regard to that which is permissible. Reason should exercise rule over desire in all this. The first instance wherein you can evidence your mastery over your desire is in eating and in drinking, just as it was in this regard that man first sinned.

Touch follows the sense of taste, and is very similar to it. Its pleasures are peculiar to those members of the body in which the humors are well balanced. There is no occasion for the reasoning soul therein, except to guide the body. As to the manner of exercising it, thou must know that these desires are ills of the body, which thou must treat, and diseases which thou must heal. Think not that it is characteristic of the intellectual soul. Do not suppose that complete happiness and perfect blessedness are to be attained thereby, as one attains to excellences, in virtue of which man is adjudged deserving of honor in matters pertaining to the intellect.

As we have entered upon a description of the senses, let us regard each of them in the light of a genus and then mention the species comprised under it, namely, the qualities of man. Then let us name every individual in the species and describe its useful and harmful qualities and the method of effecting its improvement.

If now we proceed to represent the qualities of the senses according to number, the result is that every sense has four qualities. We would attribute, firstly, to the sense of sight four, and a like number to the other senses, so that the sum would amount to twenty qualities for the five senses. Accordingly, we assign to the eye Pride, Meekness, Pudency, and Impudence. Our reason for putting pride in connection with the sense of sight is clear, as has been remarked above, while treating of it; also because thou perceivest the haughty glance of the proud and boastful of spirit. The very reverse of that we behold in the lowly of spirit, that is, meekness. Scripture says with reference to the unduly lofty, "The lofty looks of men shall be humbled," and again, "The eyes of the lofty shall be humbled," and so forth.

The use here of (the word) "eyes" shows that the quality of pride is to be attributed to the sense of sight. Of meekness it is said, "Thou art of humbler eyes than to behold evil," and so forth. With regard to the impudent, thou observest in most cases that his eyes stare and he is indifferent to shame; thus, it is said of them, "The shew of their countenance doth witness against them." Thus, thou wilt notice that the eyes of the unrighteous, the impudent, are troubled and restless, like those of whom it is said, "The eyes of the wicked shall fail." Again, it is said of the impudent, "They have made their faces harder than as rock." On the other hand, thou wilt find that the prudent man lowers his eyes so that he may merit, by reason of this, the abundant favor of God and men, as it is said , "He giveth grace unto the lowly"; and as we, with the help of God, exalted be He, will explain very clearly in the successive chapters. This favor can be acquired only by means of (the faculty of) sight, having regard to him that sees and that which is seen. Thus it was said of Moses our Master, peace be unto him, "The man Moses was very meek." Previously it was said, corresponding to this, "The man Moses was very great."

The sense of hearing constitutes a genus embracing four species, namely, four qualities - Love, Hate, Mercy, and Hard-heartedness (cruelty). One has need of great precision in determining the relation of these four qualities to the sense of hearing. Even though we do not make our exposition thoroughly clear, nevertheless men of understanding will be content with hints and allusions. He ought not to be blamed who brings forward a fraction of the truth for not gathering together the whole. Perhaps the reader will admit as excuse for me, in that I have not succeeded in bringing together the metaphysical and logical proofs and the Scriptural examples as far as I have gone, the fact that human power is but slight, especially in the case of a man like me, who is always greatly troubled and who does but scantily realize his hopes.

In some places in the Bible (a mention of) the hearing occurs, followed by urging; thus the expression, "Hear, O Israel," and after that it is said, "Thou shalt love the Lord thy God," etc. Furthermore, "When Abraham's servant heard "; it is said immediately following, "He who worshiped the Lord, bowing himself to the earth "; and again, "And it came to pass that when Laban heard the tidings, he embraced him and kissed him."

Hearing is also used in connection with acceptance and approval, which are at the basis of love; thus it is written, "We will do and we will hear." The performance of a thing is due to the love of a man therefore; thus, it is said, "Make me savoury meat, such as I love."

Sometimes satisfaction and cheerfulness follow upon hearing: thus it is said, "When Moses heard that he was content," just as anger ensues in the absence of assent and hearkening, as, "Notwithstanding, they hearkened not unto Moses." ..."And Moses was angry with them." Hatred also results from hearing, as thou must know from the case of Esau, of whom it is said, "When Esau heard," and then follows, "Esau hated Jacob." Mercy is known to result from "hearing"; thus God said, "I will hear, for I am merciful." It is said of the righteous dead, "Whoever hearkeneth unto me shall dwell safely." In contrast to this, it is said of the unrighteous, "A sound of fright is in his ears: in peace the despoiler shall come upon him," and so forth. Hard-heartedness results from the want of assent; thus it is said of Pharaoh in many places, "The Lord hardened the heart of Pharaoh and he hearkened not." A hard-hearted people is called, "A nation whose tongue thou shalt not understand, neither shalt thou hearken unto what it speaketh," and so forth.

The sense of smell also commands four qualities - Anger, Good-will, Jealousy, and Wide-awakedness. Anger is attributed to the sense of smell, as it is said, "And his nose (anger) was kindled": anger, indignation, and wrath appear mostly in connection with the nose, as it is said, "Then was Nebuchadnezzar full of fury, and the form of his nose (visage) was changed." Good-will consists in the tranquility of the thoughts, which are in the brain, and it is not altered by an "illness" of the sense of smell, though the nearest among the senses affecting it. Concerning good-will it is said, "In the light of the king's nose (countenance) is life, and his favor is as a cloud of the latter rain."

Jealousy and wide-awakedness are of the sense of the

nose, and jealousy is a branch of anger: thus, it is written, "For jealousy is the rage of a man." Thus becomes clear the association of the heated temperament, which is anger, with jealousy in the matter of this sense. Wide-awakedness consists in the movements of a man and results from the ordering of the organs of breathing, which are pivotal to the sense of smell, as we have remarked above in the section devoted to the exposition of the passage beginning with "The race is not to the swift."

The sense of taste includes as its species four qualities, namely, Joy (Cheerfulness), Grief (Apprehensiveness), Penitence, and Tranquility. Dost thou not see that the greatest pleasure is derived through eating and drinking, which is attained by means of the sense of taste? Hast thou not heard of the saying on the part of Isaac, "Bring it here unto me and I will eat of my son's venison"; and also, "And when Boaz had eaten and drunk, his heart was merry." Speech, consisting as it does of words, which are of a kind with (the objects of) taste, sometimes gives rise to joy; thus it is said, "A man hath joy by the answer of his mouth." Opposed to this we find that grief follows upon the failure to exercise this sense, as it is said, "She wept and did not eat." It is also related of Jonathan, "He did eat no meat the second day of the month, for he was grieved for David." Many such expressions are used with reference to Saul and others.

As to the quality of penitence, the reason for referring it to (the sense of) taste is that contrition and penitence are felt for what has gone before, and one denies himself different kinds of enjoyment, which are rendered possible by means of the taste, as it is said , "O Israel, return." The attributing also of the quality of tranquility to (the sense of) taste is seen in the saying of Sennecherib, "Eat ye every man of his own vine, and every one of his fig-tree;" and again, "And they saw the people that were therein, how they dwelt in safety."

The sense of touch also stands in relation to four qualities, and these are Liberality, Niggardliness, Valor, and Cowardice. Liberality in connection with touch is possible only through the action of the hand. Liberality consists in open-handedness, even as niggardliness is but close-fistedness. With regard to giving, it is said, "A man's gift maketh room for him, and before great men it will lead him." Of niggardliness, it is said, "He that gathereth by close hand will increase." That valor is in connection with the touch is evident from the connection between seizing hold of (something) and the hand; thus it is said, "Her hand she put forth to the nail." In opposition to this, it is said of cowardice, "Strengthen ye weak hands"; and again, "All hands shall become feeble," and so forth.

It having been made clear that all the qualities of the soul are related to the five senses, let us now return to our first theme (the elucidation of) which we have stated to be the purpose of this book. Seeing that most men are not sufficiently versed in the ruling of their qualities to enable them to regulate these according to ethical standards and a rational method, we have resolved to write a satisfactory treatise concerning this, which shall contain an account in extenso of the qualities, the ways in which to use them, and the mode in which to bring about their improvement. In addition to this I have met with the persistent importunity of one of my friends, who desires this as a memorial and preparation for himself and for me, in the event that conditions change in the course of time, places become disturbed and men alter. He desires also that the relationship of the qualities to the senses should be set forth. Before explaining this at all, I will make it clear to him by means of a geometrical diagram and visible proofs.

Then let us first sketch a diagram of the four temperaments, which we have mentioned above. We have drawn it at the beginning of our work, in the form of a figure, so that the imagination may be quick to grasp it and the senses ready to comprehend it. We have indicated with reference to every temperament whatever are its elements, and then joined to every temperament five qualities, in accordance with the requirements of the calculation. We have joined them to whatever quality they have, in preference to any other, after having classified them in the diagram, giving those which are hot and cold, and to which of the elements they belong, and likewise those that are moist (humid) and dry (arid) and their conjunctions and disjunctions - all this in the diagram. Of God we pray that He may put an end to the opposition (clamor) of those who, on the strength of their knowledge, enter upon a discussion with us, and that He silence the mouths of those who argue with us in their folly. I have no reason to trust that their envy will not lead them to attempt to humiliate us; yet will I not be deterred by their disturbance, nor dismayed by their brutishness. The Lord sufficeth as my portion, and in Him I trust, for He is a shield to those taking refuge with Him, the surest protection to those seeking after His help, as it is written, "The Lord is good unto them that wait for Him." Verily, I am innocent of that wherewith they charge me if they speak haughtily: I am too pious to be the victim of their pride, even though they occupy the foremost place, for there is no iniquity in my hand. Therefore, will I bear their attacks; but I do say, "They hate me only because I pursue the good."

God knows that I have not admitted into my work anything except my own thoughts and writing, nor have I busied myself with anything outside of my own ideas. To those who have superior souls and lofty aspirations, their strong affection for our discourse will point out that which we have in mind; and if they alight upon any mistakes in the course of it, they will allow that my excuse is clear and evident, since in its chief parts there is good sense.

This is a copy of the first diagram, which represents the elements and the temperaments:

We have arranged to refer every temperament to its element and every quality to its temperament, as required by the argument, which we shall make clear in another place with the help of the Almighty, the Sufficient, may

He be exalted. Having sketched this diagram as just explained, we would say here that the sum of the human qualities which we can enumerate is twenty, of which some are praiseworthy per se, and others blameworthy per se. Whosoever wishes to attain to the improvement of his qualities must pursue in his own person the goodly course so that the praiseworthy qualities come to be to him excellences, unto which he must accustom himself, from which he must not separate from the time of his youth, and whereunto he must apply himself step by step and little by little. Thus, saith the sage, "Train up a child in the way he should go, and when he is old, he will not depart from it." The philosopher hath said, "Intelligence is a gift, moral conduct is an acquirement, but habit is master over all things."

Know thou that all the qualities of man, of the possession of which he gives evidence at the period of his youth and manhood, are in him during his infancy and boyhood: though it be not in his power to manifest them, they are nevertheless within him in potential, (if) not in actu. Thou wilt observe that in some boys the quality of prudency manifests itself, and in others impudence; some incline to enjoyment, others aspire to virtue, and still others are disposed to vices; these qualities above mentioned and others similar to them being among those of the animal soul; and when men reach unto the stage of maturity, the strength of the rational soul displays its activity and it directs him that possesses it to a proper understanding with regard to the improvement of the qualities, since it is not the practice of the animal soul to improve these. Now in addition to this proposition being susceptible of proof, it has been handed down to us by tradition in the words of the Saint, "Even a child is known by his doings." As to the youths whom baseness overcomes, it is possible to transform them into a noble state as long as the limits of childhood have not been passed; but if they overstep the boundaries of youth and reach maturity, and continue to remain in this condition, it becomes difficult to set them along a good course, just as a sprig may be made to stand erect before it is full grown; but when it has become a tree, it is difficult to bend or move it. From this thou seest that most men when they have reached maturity cannot be turned aside from the course which in their youth they pursued, whereas most men can be directed between the periods of childhood and youth unto good habits. This is the simple meaning of, "Train up a child in the way he should go, and when he is old," etc.

Thus, too, our Rabbis say, "At twenty years of age, one dies with it." It is impossible that evil-doing should belong to the rational soul by nature, for this would not be in accordance with wisdom. The Deity hath created the soul pure, stainless, and simple, as saith the sage, "This only have I found, that God hath made man upright." Whatever results therefrom that is not good, is the work of the vegetative soul, i.e., the natural impulse. A philosopher has said that, "He who clings to good qualities in order to enjoy by means of them the pleasures of his senses and (to satisfy) the necessities of his body, does not understand their true value; but he understands them who seeks after them, because he recognizes their merit and usefulness and knows that death caused by following them is better than life, based upon their opposites; and he who keeps his thoughts away from the base, lifts them up to the good."

In the measure in which man separates himself from baseness does he near God, may He be exalted; and in the measure in which he nears baseness, does he separate himself from Him. Now in regard to the twenty qualities of man, David, peace be upon him, points to them and alludes to their origin in the "Psalm of David" "Contend not with thyself because of evil-doers." Of some of these he clearly treats, as may be gathered from the literal interpretation of the verse; others he indicates merely by allusions: viz., he enjoins serving God, by cultivating qualities that are praise-worthy, and inhibits the exercise of the blameworthy qualities. Furthermore, he condemns the course of those who depart from the right way, as it should be observed, and praises the course of those who rightly habituate themselves to good practice.

In saying at first, "Contend not with thyself because of evildoers," he would put an inhibition upon envy of the wicked; for, if man does not envy them, he is necessarily bound to hate them. Moreover, he warns against envy of them and jealousy of their condition, these being his words, "Be not envious against the workers of iniquity." He enjoins trustfulness in the Lord and confidence in Him, in saying, "Trust in the Lord and do good."

Furthermore, he alludes to the exercise of the qualities of prudency and modesty, "So shalt thou dwell in the land and feed in faithfulness." His saying, first, "So shalt thou dwell in the land," and then "and feed in faithfulness," shows that long life on earth is the result of cultivating humility and prudency, which he calls "faith," as thou knowest from the saying, "He is faithful in all my house," and that which preceded in the description of modesty. That which we have said of the meriting of life, even long life on earth, corresponds to the expression, "The meek shall inherit the earth." In saying, "Delight thyself also in the Lord," he alludes to the quality of joy, which the righteous exercises in that service of the Lord, wherein he delights. Thus, he says elsewhere, "Be glad in the Lord and rejoice, O ye righteous"; again, he says of the season of gladsome tidings, "I will greatly rejoice in the Lord." In saying, "He shall give thee the desires of thine heart," he alludes to the quality of yearning which is love, for God satisfies the yearning of the righteous, as is promised them in the saying, "The Lord will fulfill all thy desires."

The words, "Cease from anger" are to be taken literally; they forbid giving way to violent anger and wrath. To "Cease from anger and forsake wrath" requires, first, the uprooting thereof, and, second, penitence for what has gone before. "The meek shall inherit the earth." These are the lowly, viewing the verse literally. In saying, "The wicked plotteth against the just and gnasheth upon him with his teeth," he alludes to the use which the wicked make of impudence and recklessness. In saying, "The Lord shall laugh at him," he means that He will destroy the impudent one and cause the righteous to rejoice in his destruction; thus, it is said, "The righteous shall rejoice when he seeketh vengeance." In saying, "The wicked have unsheathed the sword," he alludes to the fervor and the daring which they (the wicked) display. In saying, "To slay such as be of upright conduct," he alludes to the quality of hard-heartedness which prevails over all their (other) qualities. In saying, "Their bows shall be broken," he hints at the quality of pride; similarly, it is said of a "brazen-faced nation", "They shall lay hold of bow and spear." In saying, "The arms of the wicked shall be broken," he means that the quality of faint-heartedness takes possession of them when their youth and strength are enfeebled, so that they cannot raise their arms at all. In saying, "The wicked borroweth and payeth not," he alludes to the quality of niggardliness. In saying, "The righteous showeth mercy and giveth," he has in mind the two qualities which dwell in the soul of the righteous, namely, mercy and liberality.

Concluding his enumeration of these qualities, he seals them with the quality of good-will. We would say that when man pursues the right course in reference to these twenty qualities, i.e., in the manner in which we have described the exercise of those that are praiseworthy, and the putting aside of those that are blameworthy, then God becomes well pleased with him, as it is said, "The steps of a good man are ordered by the Lord." Let not man suppose that the passage, "The steps of a good man are ordered by the Lord" implies any compulsion to obedience (to God) or disobedience; (it does point) however, to the bliss and misery (which are their respective reward and punishment). In saying, "The steps of a good man are ordered by the Lord," he means that God created his soul perfect, not wanting in anything; and when it inclines to virtue, to wholesome practice and good conduct, the expression "are ordered" implies that he merits the approval of God; and this is meant by the expression, "And He delighteth in his way." As a result of what we have said, it is clear that David, peace be upon him, in these hints, gives a description of the way in which to improve the qualities of the human soul and to accustom it to virtuous practice in the same manner as Solomon the Wise has done in his writings, wherein he urges (men) to affect their improvement in every possible manner, as I shall indicate, please God, exalted may He be.

Following our argument, we shall proceed to describe the method of the diagram, which we have drawn, of the senses and the qualities, and (in the course of the description), we will explain how the qualities originate in the senses, uniting every individual to its species, and every species to its genus, i.e., we will make clear the nature of the qualities derived from the sense of sight and their quantity; so also those derived from the sense of hearing, and the remaining senses in the same way. It will be a tabular diagram, so that it may easily be grasped by beginners in the study of this science, and those desirous of procuring the benefit thereof, those asking help of God in order that they may bring about their improvement, with the help of abstract (exact) and concrete (worldly) sciences.

This is the form of the tabular diagram, which is devised in order to illustrate the branching forth of the twenty qualities from the five senses.

Sight, Pride, Meekness, Prudency, Impudence, Hearing, Love, Hate, Mercy, Hard-heartedness (Cruelty), Smell, Wrath, Good-will (Suavity), Jealousy, Wideawakedness, Taste, Touch, Joy (Cheerfulness), Liberality, Grief (Apprehensiveness), Niggardliness, Tranquility, Valor, Penitence (Remorse), Cowardice.

Having attained what, we desired in the matter of the representation of the figures, let us now conclude this introduction to our work by enumerating its divisions and its chapters. We have named our work,

The Improvement of the Qualities

for the benefit largely of the masses, in order that they may gain a knowledge of the nature of the noble, and understand this matter through various methods of expression (illustration). We have introduced in the following whatever logical and demonstrable arguments have occurred to us; and, furthermore, as far as we are able, have adduced Scriptural verses. Nor, after first giving these, do I see any harm in briefly citing some utterances of the wise; and I shall follow this by adorning (what I have said) with "rejez" verses of litterateurs, and some verses from the poets, and anything uncommon that occurs to me, and whatever else I can recall, so that my book may be complete in all its parts. Perhaps the reader of this will, in his magnanimity and highmindedness, excuse my not having exhausted my theme, for my aim in composing this book was not to benefit him who surpasses me in talent at this time, since I do not lay claim, God forbid, to superiority in any department of science. Verily, the fruit which I have plucked from wisdom is my knowledge that I am not wise, that I must not abandon the counsel of my contemporaries, and that I must acknowledge to them my weakness.

I would be, in that case, as the saying goes, "as one who tends a garden well when it is in its full bloom; or like one who heaps up brocaded stuffs boastfully in the presence of those who make them." The clearest ground for excusing me, in that I have not exhausted my theme, and the surest reason for omitting to blame me for not having completed it to the very end, is that we live at the present time amid evil and distress, an uninterrupted succession of troubles and disquieting circumstances; but I complain not. Despite this, I do not cease to praise our Creator, exalted may He be, for the grace which He has vouchsafed to us, and for having enlightened our understanding and our judgment, causing us to find the way in which to comprehend something of the sciences.

I have divided my work into five parts, every part containing four chapters, which makes a total of twenty chapters, the number contained in the diagram. To every part I have joined the sense belonging to it, and to every sense whatever quality belong to it. These are the parts of the work, to wit, five, corresponding to the five senses already mentioned.

PART 1
The sense of sight, containing four chapters.
Chapter 1.   Treating of the quality of pride.
Chapter 2.   Treating of the quality of meekness, and urging the exercise thereof.
Chapter 3.   Treating of prudency and modesty.
Chapter 4.   Treating of impudence and the refraining therefrom.

PART 2
The sense of hearing, comprising four chapters.

Chapter 1. Treating of love and the methods of exercising it.

Chapter 2. Treating of hate, the thrusting aside thereof, and the abandonment of any leaning toward it.

Chapter 3. Treating of the quality of mercy and compassion, the praise of those possessed of it, and the encouragement to choose it.

Chapter 4. Treating of the quality of hard-heartedness and the relinquishment of any leaning toward it.

PART 3

The sense of taste, comprising four chapters.

Chapter 1. Treating of the quality of joy and the methods of exercising it.

Chapter 2. Treating of grief and consolation for sorrow.

Chapter 3. Treating of tranquility.

Chapter 4. Treating of penitence and guarding against (the need of) it.

PART 4

The sense of smell, containing four chapters.

Chapter 1. Treating of the quality of anger and wrath.

Chapter 2. Treating of good-will and cheerfulness.

Chapter 3. Treating of jealousy and envy.

Chapter 4. Treating of the quality of wide-awakedness.

PART 5

The sense of touch, embracing four chapters: thus, completing the twenty chapters of the book.

Chapter 1. Treating of liberality and generosity.

Chapter 2. Treating of the quality of niggardliness and the dispraise thereof.

Chapter 3. Treating of valor and the exercise thereof.

Chapter 4.   Treating of cowardice and the guarding against it.

Having finished numbering the parts of the book and its chapters, let us now begin to explain it all, with the help of God, exalted may He be. We pray that He lead us in the paths of rectitude, and by His grace bring us near unto the ways of uprightness. Thus, His Saint besought Him, "Lead me in Thy truth."

Chapter 1

TREATING OF PRIDE

How good it is that this chapter happens to be the first of all the chapters, as required by the connection.

For I have seen many of the elect exercise this quality unnecessarily and give it preference over their other qualities; so much so, that the masses take it unto themselves and make use of it in cases where it is needless to do so, until it gains the upper hand over their nature. I also observe this quality frequently present in young men, That is, in the child and the youth, especially if the temperament happen to be "yellow-hot." For it is characteristic of the yellow gall to rise. In its excitement it accustoms the nature of man to exercise this quality until he almost comes to exercise it amid circumstances unsuited to its appearance.

Among the special branches of this quality are vanity (presumptuousness), boastfulness, and haughtiness. These are not (included) among the qualities of the ancient saints, of whom their noble virtues testified that they were opposed to them.

Now, as we see, some men, who were known to exercise these qualities out of place, have thereby become despicable. Others aim to exercise the praiseworthy aspects of the quality of Pride, and are praised therefore. I shall not go to the length of recounting their names, for they are well known. This being so, we must carefully consider how to acquire the means of exercising this quality in the right place, and subduing it out of season; and we must make mention of the loathing, which ensues as a result of its blameworthiness.

When we perceive this quality beginning to affect the nature of a man, it becomes necessary for us to call his attention to serious matters, such as lead to reflection on the origin of existent things and their end, That is, the coming into being of things, their beginnings, their transitoriness, and their destruction. When he learns that all existent things are changeable, and finally that his own being will change (waste away) and his body become extinct, then the quality of his soul, which was haughty throughout the course of his life, will become meek and penitent at (the thought of) death. Since we are forced to accept this logical conclusion and traditional reasoning, it behooves the wise man to avoid preferring this quality of his own free will, since it is detestable and there results no benefit whatever from pursuing it. On the contrary, it is the cause of many dangers, especially if man's arrogance urge him not to incline to the advice of any man; and although in (seeking) advice is the essence of good counsel, he turn away from it and abide by his own opinion. Of such a man Solomon the Wise, peace be upon him, said, "The way of a fool is right in his own eyes." Thou knowest also what befell Korach and Rehoboam and others like them, who cared only for their own opinion.

Man must remember that if he realize not his own sins but consider his course correct, there will surely befall him what befell them. Concerning this the sage saith, "All the ways of a man are clean in his own eyes, but the Lord weigheth the spirit";

And he saith of pride, "Pride goeth before destruction," Namely, the result of pride and pomp is overthrow and degradation.

Thus it happened to Pharaoh, who said, "Who is the Lord?" and Goliath when he spake, "I defy the armies of Israel;" and Sennacherib for his boastfulness in saying, "Who are they among all the gods of the countries "; and Nebuchadnezzar in that he said, "Who is that God that shall deliver you out of my hands?" and others who follow them in the manner of their speech and whose end was complete abasement and utter obscurity. Whosoever is in this state is not secure from error and sin. Thus, saith the sage, "Proud and haughty scorner is his name." He mentions craftiness, because it is the source of boastfulness.

Whoever acts in this wise ought to be ashamed, and remember that according to the measure of his superciliousness will he experience contempt, and in proportion to his power will humiliation suddenly befall him. Thus, the sage saith, "A man's pride shall bring him low," For Example, boastfulness and arrogance are the main causes of man's humiliation, and these, by my life, are characteristic of the wicked, as he saith, " A high look and a proud heart."

Some of the proud vaunt themselves in the exercise of this blameworthy quality, because they delight therein (and try to excuse themselves by) arguing, that the soul inclines to distinction, and finds lowliness irksome. Again, they hold that domineering (supremacy) strengthens it, while submission weakens it, and were there no domination, the world would not be well adjusted. They further say that the prayers of the excellent had the attainment thereof in view when they said, "Let people serve thee and nations bow down to thee."

Yea, in this way God distinguished His prophet when He spoke to him, "And kings shall come out of thy loins." On the other hand, he punished those who deserved punishment by humbling their power; thus it is said, "Therefore the Lord will cut off from Israel head and foot, branch and rush in one day," and so forth. Simpletons, discussing this superciliousness, do not consider that, when they resort thereto, their souls become unduly great, that they overstep their bounds, become overbearing toward their relatives, turn away from their companions, deride the advice of every man, for as much as they rely upon their own opinions and go their own way. But when it is so exercised as to keep one away from baseness, to enable one to rise unto the excellences, and to be firm in devotion to God, exalted be He, which is His highest gift, exalted and magnified may He be, to His servants, then this becomes the means whereby men gain the grace of God and reach the everlasting kingdom. Of these it is said, "He withdraweth not his eyes from the righteous, but with kings are they on the throne; yea, he doth establish them forever, and they are exalted."

But he, who resorts to superciliousness unnecessarily and takes only his own counsel, is like him of whom it was said, "He intermeddleth with all wisdom." Men disregard such a man and desire not his presence: of such as these the sage saith, "The sluggard is wiser in his own conceit than seven men that can render a reason." And often, moreover, his vanity impels him to undertake something outside of his usual course of action, because he relies upon his opinion saving him and upon his counsel protecting him. It is this that causes him to stumble; thus, it is said, "He disappointeth the devices of the crafty, so that their hands cannot perform their enterprise."

Having progressed thus far in our description of the quality of superciliousness, the way in which to make use thereof moderately, and the mode of suppressing its use in the wrong place, we must now proceed to quote very sparingly a few prose utterances of the wise concerning this quality, and whatever verses concerning it we can.

The divine Socrates said: "From whom doth disappointment never part? He who seeks a rank for which his ability is too feeble." Again he said, "He who sets himself up as wise will be set down by others for a fool." I hold that bad manners are attributable to superciliousness. Socrates said, "aversion is always felt for him who has an evil nature, so that men flee away from him." Aristotle says, "As the beauty of form is a light for the body, so is beauty of character a light for the soul." Again, he said in his testament to Alexander his pupil," It does not show much nobility of purpose on the part of a king to lord it over men; (the less so) for one man over a fellow-man."

A certain haughty man is said to have been journeying along with his effects; some of them fell down, whereupon he threw the others out of the wagon. The ancients say, "With him who is pleased with himself, many become displeased." A poet composed these lines concerning the blame-worthiness of haughtiness and arrogance: "Let him who shows great vanity concerning his beauty consider this! If men would but consider what is within them, neither young nor old would feel proud. Are there not in the head of every son of man five orifices from which come forth effluvia? The nose exudes, the ear gives forth an unpleasant odor, the eye sheds tears, and the mouth salivates. O son of earth, to be consumed of earth on the morrow, desist from thy pride, for thou wilt be food and drink (to the earth)! " It is told of Ardeshir, the king, that he gave a book to a man accustomed to stand at his side, and said unto him, "When thou seest me become violently angry give it to me," and in the book (was written), "Restrain thyself, for thou art not God; thou art but a body, one part of which is on the point of consuming the other, and in a short while it will turn into the worm and dust and nothingness."

Chapter 2

TREATING OF MEEKNESS

This quality is more nearly a virtue than that which was mentioned just before, because the possessor of this attribute, i.e., modesty and humility, withholds his desire from seeking gratification. When one attains this precious rank, the praiseworthy character in man is made perfect. This, in my opinion, is a disposition which merits praise for him who acquires it. Verily, he is accorded the loftiest praise.

Dost thou not see that humility is the highest degree of the nobles and of the prophets, distinguished by their divine rank? One of them said, "I am but dust and ashes "; another said, "I am a worm and no man"; and so forth. They were praised for their actions and were honored. A man of intelligence should know that lowliness and meekness cause him to realize his desire in regard to present things, as thou knowest from the account of what happened to the captains of Achaziah, because of their folly; and what happened to the third captain who gently spake, "I pray thee let my life and the life of these thy fifty servants be precious in thy sight." Him there befell the reverse of what had befallen the former. Verily, fame and glory will be the reward of whosoever is lowly. The recompense of meekness is honor and prosperity, and also the deserving of honor. Thus it is said, "The reward of humility and the fear of God are riches, and honor, and life."

The most excellent of the ancient nobles (may God guide thee aright) were accustomed to exercise the quality of meekness, and preferred it to their natural impulses. It is related of an illustrious king, that one night while a number of people were assembled about him, he arose to trim the lamp. Whereupon it was said to him, "Why didst thou not utter a command, which would have sufficed?" And he answered them, "As king I rose, and as king I resume my seat."

He was wont to say that "Every grace (of man) is envied, except meekness." The philosopher Buzurjmih said, "The fruits of lowliness are love and tranquillity." Know thou that in honoring his brother or his neighbor, man honors himself. Someone has remarked that "lowliness consists in being beforehand with greetings to whomsoever one may meet, and in descending to the lowest rank." Contentment is of a kind with this quality.

When one is gifted with its presence, he has already gained superiority. It is said, "Whomsoever the Lord loveth he inspireth with contentment." Scripture says of the contented servant of God, "The righteous eateth to the satisfying of the soul." And it says of the reverse, "But the belly of the wicked shall want." He who possesses strength, health, and a sense of security ought never to feel sad. The fruit of contentment is tranquility. The greatest riches are contentment and patience.

One of the sages has said, "He who desires of this world only that which is sufficient for him, will be content with the very least thereof." Another sage was wont to admonish his son, "He who cannot bear with one word, will be compelled to listen to many. He who esteems his rank but slightly, enhances men's estimation of his dignity." In holding the view that it may be right (at times) to repudiate this quality, I mean thereby that a man should not abase himself before the wicked. With reference to such a case it is said, "A righteous man, falling down before the wicked, is as a troubled fountain and a corrupt stream." It was said concerning this, "He who deserves (the greatest) compassion is the wise man lost among fools. "In the ethical sayings of Lokman (we find), " When the noble man forsakes the world, he becomes humble: the ignoble in forsaking the world becomes haughty." In the book of al-Kuti (it is said), "Be humble without cringing, and manly without being arrogant. Know thou that arrogance is a wilderness and haughtiness a taking refuge therein, and, altogether, a going astray."

Chapter 3

ON THE QUALITIES OF PRUDENCY AND MODESTY

A wish man was asked, "What is intelligence?" and he answered, "Modesty." Again, he was asked, "What is modesty?" and he replied, "Intelligence."

This quality, although like unto meekness and agreeing therewith, is of a nobler rank than the latter, for it is kindred to intelligence. To every man of understanding the nobility of the intellect is patent, for it is the dividing line between man and beast, in that it masters man's natural impulses and subdues passion. With the help of intelligence man realizes the benefit of knowledge and gets to understand the true nature of things; he comes to acknowledge the Unity of God, to worship his Master, and to bear a striking resemblance to the character of the angels.

Since this precious quality is of so noble a kind, it follows that modesty which resembles it is almost equally so. The proof of its being thus related is, that thou wilt never see a modest man lacking intelligence, or an intelligent man devoid of modesty.

This being so, man must direct all his efforts to the attainment of this wonderful and highly considered quality. He must prefer it to all his natural impulses, and regard it as superior to all his other qualities, for by means of it he acquires many virtues, and all vice becomes hidden from him. Thus it is said, "The faults of him, whom modesty clothes with dignity, will not be remarked by men." Dignity and honor follow upon him. Thus it is said, "Before honor is humility." The meek find acceptance before God because of their modesty; He brings them unto everlasting bliss. Concerning him who understands its ways, it is said, "The meek will He guide in judgment: and the meek will He teach His way." Even as it is necessary that the intelligent man be prudent in the presence of others, so must he be prudent when alone. It was said that, "Prudency and faith are interdependent, and either cannot be complete without the other." A poet said, "Keep guard over thy modesty: truly prudency marks the countenance of a nobleman." It is said that "Impudence and a lack of prudency are offshoots of unbelief." He who wishes to acquire prudency should associate with those who are modest with respect to him.

An Arab was wont to say, "Pay no regard to any man unless he show thee that he cannot do without thee, even when thou needest him most, so that, if thou sin, he will forgive and act as though he were the sinner; and, if thou wrong him, he will demean himself as though he had been the offender." Another said, "Finally, one learns from the words of prophecy, 'If thou art not prudent, do whatsoever thou wilt.'" In the course of a characterization of modesty, the poet said, "Upon him reposes the mantel of piety: and, in truth, a light streams from between his eyes." Al-fadil says: "By reason of belief and piety, men dwell together for a time. Afterward they are kept together by reason of modesty, prudency, and blamelessness." Aristotle said in his discourse, "As a result of modesty (one's) helpers are multiplied."

He was accustomed to say, "In chaste children modesty clearly rules over their countenance." It was termed prudency only because it is the way to eternal life. A philosopher said, "Modesty asserts itself in the midst of wrath." Again, it was said, "The enmity of the modest man is less harmful to thee than the friendship of the fool." He who desires to guard this quality should not trifle away his dignity when asked to serve men, for when thou hast once worn out thy dignity, thou wilt find no one to renew it for thee.

To make use of prudency (that is, to be over prudent), in speaking the truth or enjoining good acts, in spreading religion and devotion, is blameworthy. In such cases one must not make use of it; thus the saint said, "I will speak of thy testimonies also before kings, and will not be ashamed." But it is necessary for man to cover his face with the mantle of modesty before all men, as thou knowest from the case of Saul when he hid himself, (as) it is written, "Behold he is hidden among the vessels." God selected him for kingship, as it is written, "Behold whom the Lord hath chosen." To sum up, according to the opinion of the philosophers and the sages, this quality is one of the virtues of the noble soul, and its relation to these is as that of the spirit to the body. A philosopher said, "Modesty consists in conducting affairs in the best way wherein it is possible for them to be conducted, and in leaving them in their best aspects." He who is modest will attain to power.

Chapter 4

TREATING OF THE QUALITY OF IMPUDENCE

We had much to say on the praiseworthiness of the quality of prudency, but the quantity of blame which we shall mete out to the quality of impudence is small. He who is possessed of the quality of shamelessness is culpable in the eyes of God, as are those of whom it is said, "They have made their faces harder than a rock; they have refused to return." The Saint says with reference to the impudent, "When pride cometh, then cometh shame," which means that when impudence prevails over the qualities of man, he is scorned by men and not respected. He is not taken seriously, nor is he regarded with that consideration for his wisdom, even though he be learned, which is paid to the prudent. Thus it is written: "But with the lowly is wisdom." If one is wise and desires to pursue the goodly course which is acceptable unto God, let him abandon this quality, refrain from exercising it, and keep it afar from the character of his soul. Of him who is impudent the prince saith, "Proud and haughty scorner is his name," by which he means that God will requite according to his doing, whosoever is impudent, as it is written, "Who dealeth in proud wrath." It is possible also that "Who dealeth in proud wrath" refers to such an impudent one as, by reason of the quality of impudence, provokes the displeasure and annoyance of others, and so forth.

When this disposition becomes part of man's nature, whosoever is familiar with him must turn him away from it by rebuking him as much as he is able, and by annoying him, until he be rid of all that was in him. Thus it is said, "A wicked man hardens his face." Yet impudence (boldness) may be commendable when supporting religion, when performing "service" and speaking the truth. But to oppose thereby the righteous and the Prophets of God is reprehensible. Thus it is said, "Impudent children and stiff- hearted." If the man who practises this quality be of a yellow (bilious) constitution, and if in the course of his youth he give strong evidence of its possession, he must oppose to it its very reverse. Let him trust in God, and he will accustom himself to avoid this blameworthy quality and subdue it.

<u>Chapter 1</u>

ON THE QUALITY OF LOVE

It is almost impossible for any man to be secure from this "accident," O God, save he whose intellect is master over his nature. None such exists; and if any (be found to) exist, he is undoubtedly one of the most excellent (men). Lust is a constituent element in the nature of man, and if he desire to be master and ruler, let him cast away lust (passion), make no use of it whatever, ignore it and do without it, for it is one of the baser qualities. It is well known that the qualities of the wise are not perfected until their souls gain the mastery over their desires. The deeds of him whose intellect prevails over his lustfulness are commendable. Upon the realization of desires, there ensues the penalty of misfortune. One of the signs of him, who is overcome by his lust, is that he is very changeable, restless, and fickle of speech. Especially if, added to this, the bloody temper prevails in his constitution and he be in the period of youth and the season of spring, then it proves too strong for him. Therefore, the wise man must shrink from this quality lest he make use of it and turn away from it, for there is connected with it no inconsiderable harm. Thou knowest how contempt, obscurity, and abasement come upon its devotee, and that finally its outcome is evil. This thou knowest from the story of Amnon and what happened to him when he hastened after his desire.

Man ought to employ this quality only in the service of God and His divine Law, as it is written, "And his delight is in the law of the Lord," and again, "How I love thy law," etc. Necessarily, one who occupies himself with the quest of knowledge and moral science (theoretical science and the practical arts), will be (so busy as to be) kept from his lusts. The wise one said, "If aught befall thee and no one occur to thee whom thou may consult with reference thereto, avoid it and bring it not near to thy passion, for passion is an enemy of the heart." And he said, "He who is submissive to his lust is routed, and he who rebels against it gains the victory." This quality is preferred by foolish men only because of the imminence (immediateness) of its delight and for the sake of the amusement and merriment and the hearing of mirthful songs which they get through it. They heed not the suffering and the wretchedness that follow in its train, and therefore incline in accord with their natural impulses to the attainment of present pleasure, as it is said, "The desire accomplished is sweet to the soul,"

turning aside from wisdom and the service of the Lord, because of what appears to be the remoteness of the delight and pleasurableness of these things. Verily, in their opinion, these are remote. Yet these are not remote, but near at hand. They are remote only in their mind. Therefore man must devote this quality of love to God, exalted may He be, as it is written, "Thou shalt love the Lord thy God"; and to his soul, as it is written, "For he loved him as he loved his own soul"; to his relatives, as it is written, "And Jacob loved Rachel"; to his offspring, as it is written , "Israel loved Joseph"; to his country, as it is written , "But I will depart to my own land and to my kindred"; to his companion, as spake David to Jonathan , "Very pleasant hast thou been unto me" ; to his wife , "Let her be as the loving hind and the pleasant roe"; to wisdom, as it is written, "The man that loveth wisdom rejoiceth his father."

The moral application of this quality is, man must evince it (in his dealings) with all men. It has been said, "He who desires to be endeared to men should conduct himself with regard to them in the best possible manner. Benefit occasions love even as injury begets hatred." Moreover, included under this quality are wishes and unattainable desires. It is right for the man of understanding that he train himself (to keep aloof) therefrom. The following is part of what the poets have said concerning such wishes as cannot be realized, and wherefrom the soul realizes naught except possibly weariness of spirit, continual disquietude, and protracted restlessness: "My day is a day which is common to men until the darkness of the night is fallen, and then my couch wearies me. I spent my day in entertainment and in desire but the night brought me altogether to grief." Among other things which have been said with reference to devoting one's self wholly to pleasure and passion, the blameworthy outcome of this, and the trouble which is associated therewith, the poet says: "We have drunk of the dregs of the wine as if we were kings of the two Iraqs and the sea; but when the sun shone brightly, thou mightest have found me with my riches flown, and poverty once more my own." When this quality obtains the mastery of the soul, the senses become blunted and man is not conscious because of his being given over to pleasure. He is as those of whom it is said , "Woe unto them that call evil good and good evil." The maxim of the sage is, "Thy love of anything renders thee blind and deaf." One sage, writing to another on the subject of subduing the lusts, said, "Thou shalt not attain what thou lovest until thou suffer much from what thou loathest. And thou shalt not be delivered from that which thou loathest, until thou suffer much through that which thou lovest."

__Chapter 2__

TREATING OF HATE

Thou shouldst know that he who hates men is hated by them, and when this quality takes firm hold of the soul, it destroys it, because it leads to the hatred of the very food and drink with which man sustains life. Besides, he suffers injury through the hostility of men. When excessive love is expended on other than divine things, it is changed into the most violent hatred. As thou knowest from the expression, "Then Amnon hated her exceedingly." He who loves thee for some reason will turn his back, simultaneously with its disappearance and ending. Thou must not trust in the counsel of the enemy, the "Hater." Thus it is written, "The kisses of an enemy are deceitful." From this quality there branches out fretfulness. Thou knowest how the prevalence of fretfulness has been censured, the blameworthiness which attaches to its use and the repugnance the soul feels therefor.

It has been said that the fretful cannot abide by one state; he has not a friend; his circumstances are always disturbed, and misery never parts company with him. He is like one of whom it is said, "The slothful (listless) man roasteth not that which he took in hunting." Thou knowest that many men make a show of friendship in their speech and yet frequently are enemies at heart. Do not trust them, as it is written, "He that hateth, dissembleth with his lips." Even though he be gentle in discourse with thee, do not associate with him, as it is written, "When he speaketh fair, believe him not." Thus Joab also made a show of kind-heartedness and affection for Abner and Amasa before killing them. So also did Ismael favor Guedaliah ben Achikam ere he killed him. It is said, "He who sows hatred will reap regret." He who is of this character is ill-disposed to his fellow-man in matters concerning himself and another. So much the more will he be so in those affecting him and his Lord. He acts as though he were praying, but his secret thoughts are quite different. Thus it is written of them, "Nevertheless they did flatter him with their mouth and they did lie unto him with their tongues," and so forth. The divine Socrates spake unto his disciples, bidding them "Beware of whomsoever your heart hates, for the hearts of men are like a mirror." Thus the sage said, "As in water, face answereth to face, so the heart of man to man." Souls are alike, and the most harmful and persistent form of hatred is that caused by envy. The poet saith, "Thou canst cure all manner of enmity except the enmity which comes to thee through envy." In the book of al-Kuti (it is said), "The very best that thou canst look forward to in regard to thy enemies is that thou bring them back to the love of thee, if that be possible."

Chapter 3

TREATING OF THE QUALITY OF MERCY AND
COMPASSION (PITY), THE PRAISE OF ITS
POSSESSORS, AND AN EXHORTATION TO GIVE
PREFERENCE THERETO. THIS FORMS THE
SEVENTH CHAPTER OF THE BOOK

Since this quality is of a kind with the nature of the
Creator, may He be greatly praised and mightily exalted,
it is complementary to the twelve attributes especially
characteristic of Him, the thirteen qualities which are
ascribed to the Lord of Worlds, viz., "The Lord eternal is
a merciful and gracious God," and so forth. That which it
is possible for the wise man to aim at in action is, being
slow to anger, "long-suffering," and largely generous, as
it is said, "abundant in loving-kindnesses," tolerant of sin,
as it is said, "Forgiving iniquity," and so forth. The
upright and wise man must emulate these as far as he is
able to do. Even as man desires that he be dealt with
mercifully, when compelled to seek help, so must he be
merciful to whosoever seeks his help. This quality is
extremely praiseworthy, and God, exalted may He be, has
distinguished His righteous servants through their love
therefore. As thou knowest of Joseph, where it is said,
"His bowels did yearn upon his brother." The intelligent
man has the qualities of pity and compassion implanted
in his soul and ever present therein.

The sage said, "Mercy is the result of kindliness and
honesty." In regard to it, Solomon the Wise spake when
he exhorted to mercy and compassion, "If thou forbear to

deliver them that are born unto death." A beautiful feature of this quality in connection with the Creator, exalted and hallowed may He be, is that He is merciful in dealing with all His creatures. Thus, it is said, "The Lord is good to all, and His tender mercies are over all His works." In the book of Al-Kuti, it is said, "Spare no effort to deliver those who are confronted with death." Again, he said, "Do not wrong the weak, for their Protector is God, the mighty One." He said, "Prosperous are they whose heart is ever merciful and meek," and again we find therein, "He who is not merciful will die by the hand of one who is merciless."

Chapter 4

TREATING OF HARD-HEARTEDNESS

I do not find this quality among righteous or superior men. But it is (to be found) in him whose nature resembles that of a lion, for he is one who is never sated. These are the ones of whom it is said, "A nation of fierce countenance." Upon my soul, this is a wholly detestable quality, whether (its measure be) great or small. It comes into being when the spirit of wrath prevails over a man. This quality is exercised for the purpose of wreaking vengeance upon enemies. There is no harm in making use of it in this manner, although the intelligent man ought not endeavor to be avenged upon his enemies. For this is not befitting. Thus, saith the sage, "Rejoice not when thy enemy falleth." To make use of it in order that one may do evil to his fellow-man, to kill him, or to lay hold of the possessions of one who has given no offence, is reprehensible. From such as these may God preserve me, for of their ilk, the Saint said, "If it had not been the Lord who was on our side, now may Israel say:" … "Then they had swallowed us up quick, when their wrath was kindled against us." A proof that this quality is only found in the wicked is the expression, "But the tender mercies of the wicked are cruel." Plato, the author of the laws in regard to vengeance, said, "He who desires to be revenged upon his enemies should add (a degree of) excellence to himself."

Chapter 1

TREATING OF JOY (CHEERFULNESS)

This quality is found to differ in various men. Sometimes, it is natural; this is the case in him whose temper is humid-hot as is that of blood; especially when his hopes are well ordered and never confounded, and who, in addition, is far from experiencing suffering and free from affliction. It is but meet that in the nature of him who is of this character there appear the sign of this quality that his exterior be sound, his health robust, and old age without haste in overtaking him. Thus, it is said of such a one, "A merry heart doeth good like a medicine, but a broken spirit dries the bones."

Sometimes it is coincident with the attainment of the desire and the realization of a wish. Peculiar to it is continual smiling without (apparent) cause. Very often lightmindedness accompanies it, whereof it is written, "For as the crackling of thorns under a pot, so is the laughter of the fool." It has been said that one of the distinguishing marks of the fool is his laughing when there is no occasion for laughter.

I hold that this quality is to be found in the souls of those, above all, who are free from defilement, the righteous, the pious, the pure, destined for the Heavenly Kingdom, rising to spirituality, i.e., the souls of the upright, for they are in perfect enjoyment of their condition of service and greatly rejoiced because of their worship, as it is written , "Be glad in the Lord and rejoice, ye righteous; and shout for joy, all ye that are upright in heart." The well-bred man ought not to indulge in laughter when seated in an assembly, for it was said that for him who laughs much, but little respect is felt. Facetiousness takes away the veil of dignity. Even as anxiety (apprehensiveness) when it is aroused gives rise to weeping, so gladness, when it is stirred, incites to laughter.

Therefore, the intelligent man ought to understand that this quality and some other qualities are not of the rational soul, as Galen holds, but of the animal soul. The proof of this is that thou seest laughter break out in spite of dreadful events. Often, too, man is unable to refrain therefrom. The same is held with regard to wrath and other qualities. Considering this, man should urgently seek to render his animal soul submissive to his rational soul: namely, that his intellect guide his nature. When he does this, he becomes included among the most excellent men. Wherefore Socrates says in regard to joy, "Whatever causes joy causes sorrow." In the ethics of Diogenes, treating of joy, he states: "Joy is life and exaltation to the heart, whereas grief is distress and destruction."

Chapter 2

TREATING OF GRIEF

This quality usually succeeds in establishing itself in the soul when wishes fail of realization, and then the soul is brought to such a point as almost to be killed when it loses the objects of its love. Oh, what a quality is this! How serious a matter when it comes into evidence, and how waste is its place when it prevails! Thus, it was said, "Apprehensiveness is a living death."

I have determined to linger here a little in the discussion of this chapter. Perhaps God will grant us His grace and inspire us with excellent words, which may relieve the sadness of man, so that he may find healing in our discourse, because it is impossible to find healing for psychical ills other than in spiritual remedies. As this takes firmer hold of the soul, so also it becomes more difficult to find the remedy. Of God we pray that He protect us therefrom in His graciousness. The constitution of apprehensiveness is cold and dry, like the black gall (humor). No man can absolutely escape it. In some it attains immense proportions, so that they thereby become afflicted with psychical ailments. Thus it is said, "Gloom in the heart of man maketh it stoop, but a good word maketh it glad." Know thou that this quality is generally visible in the countenance, as thou hast seen in the case of Joseph, who discerned what was in the heart of " the servants of Pharaoh," when he beheld their austere countenances; it being said, "And he looked upon them, and behold they were sad," and as Artaxerxes said to

Nehemiah, "Why is thy countenance sad, seeing thou art not sick." Thus, it is obvious that this quality is generally distinctly visible in the countenance.

Thou shouldst know that if a man be madly in love with this world, which is a world de generatione et corruptione, he never omits to seek the gratification of the senses, constantly moving on from one thing to another. If he attain them and then lose them, gloom overcomes him. On the other hand, if he be made to forget this world, and apply himself to the world of intellect, then it becomes possible for him to escape the psychical ills, which are (occasioned by) worldly acquisitions, that is, if he turn away from vain works and incline in the fulness of the soul to ethical science and religious laws. Therefore, the intellectual man ought to cast away the lowly quality of the masses and the grandiose manner of kings.

If it be impossible for a man to have what he desires, he must desire what he has. Let him not prefer continual gloom. We ought to strive to cure our souls of this evil (disease), in the same way as we must suffer hardships in trying to cure our bodies and to rid them of diseases by means of burning and cutting (fire and iron), and so forth. Rather must we gradually accustom ourselves to improve our souls through strength of purpose, and to endure a little difficulty in order that, as a result of this, we may pursue a praiseworthy course. We know, moreover, that if we represent to ourselves that no misfortune will befall us, it is as though we desired not to exist at all. Because misfortunes are a necessary condition of the passing of worldly things. If this were not, there could be no becoming. Ergo, to wish that no accident should come to pass is like wishing not to exist. But existence is (a part) of nature, and annihilation likewise is (a part) of nature. Then if we desire that this be not (a part) of nature, we desire the impossible; he who desires the impossible will have his wish denied, and he whose wish is denied is miserable.

We ought to be ashamed to give the preference to this quality, grief, and we should yearn to rise unto a state of beatitude. Let him who would not mourn represent to his soul the things that lead to mourning, as though they already were; thus, for example, let man say, "A certain possession of mine will be destroyed and I will mourn for it," accounting it as already destroyed, or (considering) as already lost that which he loves. Concerning this, the poet-philosopher said: "The man of prudence grows up, representing to himself his mishaps before they befall him; if they befall him suddenly, they will not terrify him because of the things already pictured in his soul. He sees that one thing will lead to another, and therefore he knows the end from the beginning." But not the least trace of apprehensiveness is to be found in those who are of lofty souls and noble aspirations. Socrates was asked, "Why do we never perceive in thee any sign of apprehensiveness?" And he answered, "Because I have never possessed anything over the loss of which I would grieve."

Wherefore let the intelligent man consider that there is nothing in this world of all that grows, save it be insignificant at the outset, and afterward develops, except grief, which is greatest on the day it comes into being, and the longer it continues the less it becomes, until it entirely disappears. The firm and resolute man is he who braces himself up with all his might in the hour of his affliction. Alexander, in order to console his mother about himself (in the event of his death), wrote to her as follows: "My mother, order a great and fortified city to be built when the news of Alexander's death reaches you. Prepare therein for eating and drinking, and gather together in it, on an appointed day, men from all the lands to eat and drink. When that has been done and all the men are ready to eat and drink what the queen has prepared, let it be proclaimed at that moment that no man should enter her abode whom misfortune has befallen." And thus she did upon the death of Alexander. But when she ordered that no one whom misfortune had befallen should enter her house, she noticed (that) no one (came). Then she felt sure that he had only wished to comfort her about himself.

Alexander had heard from Aristotle, his master, that "Grief injures the heart and destroys it." He wished to ascertain the truth of this. He therefore decided upon an animal, the nature of which was nearest to that of man, confined it in a dark place, and allotted to it nourishment only sufficient to sustain its body. Afterward he led it forth and slaughtered it: whereupon he found its heart dissolved and melted away. Then he knew that Aristotle had spoken nothing but the truth.

Among the words spoken by Galen on grief (we find), "Apprehensiveness is a consuming of the heart, and sadness is a sickness of the heart." Afterward he explained this, saying, "Sadness is felt for what is past, and apprehensiveness for what may occur." In another place again (he said), "Sadness (is occasioned) by what has occurred, and apprehensiveness is (felt) for what may come to pass. Therefore beware of sadness, for sadness is the end of life." Dost thou not see that when the face of man is overclouded (with sadness), he will perish of grief.

One of the sages said, "Drinking poison is easier (to endure) than apprehensiveness." Now, if one should ask what benefit is derived from choosing this quality at the occurrence of misfortune and its appearance, I would answer that in shedding the tears which have become spoiled and stagnant, and which nature is incapable of returning to their place, we pour out the putrid humors, which have become rotten, the chyme, and we remedy it through purifying drugs, and thus we cleanse the humor in such a manner as to cause it to return to its original state. Thus it is known that in some small children there is a spoiled excess, which cannot be passed off save through weeping. This, then, is the natural use of weeping. Wherefore Socrates said, "Sorrows are a species of ills of the heart, as diseases are ills of the body." Among the words of Ptolemy on this (subject are), "Let him who wishes to live long, prepare to meet misfortunes with a patient heart."

Chapter 3

TREATING OF TRANQUILITY

This quality is commendable when a man directs it in faith in the Lord, and places his reliance and his confidence in Him. Thus it is said, "That thy trust may be in the Lord." This is a praiseworthy disposition: its possessor is worthy of very good fortune and abundant mercy from God, as it is written, "He that trusteth in the Lord, mercy shall compass him about." He who is in this state deserves to be blest, as it is said, "Blessed is the man that trusteth in the Lord and whose hope the Lord is." This quality is usually found in the upright, those who fear God and who are referred to in the command, which declares, "Ye that fear the Lord, trust in the Lord." The excellence of this quality and its merit before God, exalted be He, (is seen in the fact that) He promised it to Jacob during his sleep, as it is said, "Fear not, O Jacob, my servant," and as it is said of the righteous man who trusts in the Lord and who confides in Him, "He shall not be afraid of evil tidings: his heart is fixed, trusting in the Lord."

Chapter 4

TREATING OF PENITENCE (REMORSE)

This quality comes into being, when a man quits a sinful state and repents. When he gives evidence of the quality of penitence, then his repentance is complete. It must be preceded by three conditions, namely, penitence, seeking pardon, and guaranteeing to abandon one's wonted course. Thus our master Saadya Alfayumi, may God be gracious unto him, explained that one of the righteous was wont to say, "He who repents of his past sins is as though he had not sinned." This trait is commendable from this point of view. But the reprehensible side of it comes to light in the case of him who says "Yes" to-day in some matter and after a time regrets what he has said and retracts, or who vows to fast or to give alms and repents of his vow. All this is blameworthy.

The reasonable way, in my opinion, is for man to beware of placing himself in a position which he may be compelled to regret. Although men have not the power so to control themselves, that they can choose (all) their qualities, nevertheless they can desire to rise gradually from a base to a lofty course, and from faulty qualities to sound ones. The acme of bliss for man is to be able to bridle his soul, to rule it, to lead it along the right way. He whose nature yields to his intellect becomes lordly; his merit becomes high and profitable, and his deeds are praised.

Chapter 1

TREATING OF WRATH

This quality, although among the forces of the animal soul, we have set down as one of the qualities of man, because of its analogy to his other qualities. Let us begin by describing its useful side, although the latter is inseparable from its baneful aspect. There is no quality so reprehensible, but that it at times serves a use, even as no quality is so praiseworthy, but that it frequently becomes detrimental. Thus thou knowest that silence is a commendable trait, but it becomes detestable when resorted to while listening to absurdities. Wrath is a reprehensible quality, but when employed to correct or to reprove, or because of indignation at the performance of transgressions, it becomes laudable. Therefore the thoroughly wise and ethically trained man must abandon both extremes and set about the right mean. Galen said in his book on the qualities of the soul, "Wrath and anger are two words with one meaning." "Sometimes it appears, (to judge) from the countenance of the wrathful, that he is distressed, his body feverishly inflamed, his heart throbbing violently, his pulse beating strongly and swiftly." He said again, "Dignity becomes apparent in him who indulges in wrath only after reflection. But he who indulges therein unadvisedly gives evidence of stupidity." Wherefore the saying, "He who is mighty in wrath and violent in anger is not far removed from the mad." In the book of Al-Kuti (it is said) that the man of wrath is never seen to be joyful.

We would classify the wrathful soul as of four kinds. He who is quickly angered and (as) quickly appeased is of an even-balanced disposition. This is mainly characteristic of a man possessed of a yellow (bilious) temperament. He who is slow to anger and difficult to appease is likewise of an even-balanced disposition. But he who is difficult to appease and quickly angered is in a reprehensible condition because he has overstepped the boundaries of moderation. But he who is slow to anger and quickly appeased is most praiseworthy. This is one of the virtues of the noble and excellent men, among whose qualities wrath rarely ever appears.

Those who subdue their souls' anger and prevail upon their nature to restrain it, have been described as noble and characterized as exalted. Thus the sage said, "He that is slow to anger is better than the mighty." This is one of the thirteen attributes ascribed to God, exalted is He, in the passage, "And the Lord passed by before him," etc. It is said that as scab is a disease of the body, so is wrath a disease of the soul. The moral man must not become wrathful often, because, by reason of his wrath, he is compelled to bear burdens. Thus, saith the sage, "A man of great wrath shall bear punishment."

The sage has forbidden it, saying, "Be not hasty in thy spirit to be angry." Furthermore the verse makes clear the reason for his forbidding it in the expression, "For anger resteth in the bosom of fools." The wrathful deserves to be called "fool." It is impossible in most cases for the man of violent wrath to be secure from grave sin and serious transgression. Thus the sage spake: "A wrathful man aboundeth in transgression." Thou wilt notice that most men, when they become wroth and violently angry, take no heed of the disaster which they may incur through the violence of their anger, like him of whom it is said , "A fool uttereth all his mind," and on the other hand . "But a wise man keepeth it till afterward." Therefore our masters, peace be upon them, sought to interdict the immoderate exercise of this quality, saying, "He who rends his garments in wrath is like unto an idolater." According to this, a superior man must not be violent in wrath, for he accustoms himself to the qualities of the wild and wicked beast. Nor must he be so gentle as never to become wrathful, for this were characteristic of little boys. The discreet stand with reference to this is to take the intermediate course. Thou must know that man's reason is perfected when it subdues his wrath. Thus Scripture says, "The discretion of a man deferreth his anger." Ptolemy, the sage, said of wrath, "When thou becomest wrathful, pardon, for if thou dost not yield, the taking of vengeance is a sign of weakness."

Chapter 2

TREATING OF THE QUALITY OF GOOD-WILL (SUAVITY)

This is one of the praiseworthy qualities, since it is rarely to be met with, except in the case of a noble-minded person, who accepts things just as they come to him and looks not for better ones. The quality of contentment is also derived therefrom. This is, as thou knowest, reader, an excellent quality, which we have portrayed and extolled above in the second chapter of Part I, whilst treating of the quality of meekness. If the righteous man be well disposed toward his fellow-men and the latter similarly disposed toward him, it is certain that he will be acceptable unto God. Yea, more, even his enemies will make peace with him. Thus the sage saith , "When a man's ways please the Lord, he maketh even his enemies to be at peace with him," as thou knowest from the goodwill Abimelech bore Abraham, peace be upon him, and the latter's making peace with him; thus also in the speech of our sainted Rabbi to R. Hiyya, and so forth.

Wherefore the excellence of good-will is related to life, being a source of superiority and a fount of good fortune according to the saying, "In the light of the king's countenance is life; and his favor is as a cloud of the latter rain." So also in that of man; thus Pharaoh bore good-will to Joseph, even bringing him unto kingly power. Thus Ahasuerus, too, bore good-will to Mordecai. Thou seest how such a man is treated and exalted; how much more he to whom God bears good-will, therefore the saying, "I am the Lord thy God which teacheth thee to profit, which leadeth thee by the way that thou shouldst go." The sage said, "Whosoever is contented is rich: whosoever is obedient is joyous: whosoever is rebellious is sad." He was wont to say, "He who is not content of his own accord with his condition will be (compelled to be) satisfied despite himself."

From this quality there branch out forbearance and forgiveness, which are of the attributes of the Creator, exalted is He and blest, and of the wise and noble man. The poet spake, "If I were not to pardon a brother's fault, and if I were to say that I would exact vengeance from him, where then would be the superiority? And if I were to cut myself from my brethren because of their sins, I would be alone, and have none with whom to associate." It is related: "A king once became angry at a company of men and commanded that they be slain. Then spake one of them, 'Verily we have sinned grievously. Will not thy goodliness manifest itself in forgiveness?' Whereupon he forgave them and slew them not."

Chapter 3

TREATING OF JEALOUSY

This quality is an offshoot of wrath. Most rational beings are not exempt from it: but it is in them all, for we see men seeking to imitate the actions of their companions. For instance, when one (man) sees that his friend has acquired some worldly gain, mineral, animal, or vegetable, or other possessions, he likewise endeavors to acquire similar things, although he be able to dispense with them or compensate himself with other things in their stead. Let him not protract his endeavor, nor set his heart upon attaining such possessions. This is the expression to which the sage, peace be upon him, gave utterance, "Again I considered all travail and every right work, that for this a man is envied of his neighbor."

He whose nature is overcome by this disposition is blameworthy, for it leads him to envy, and a noble man is never found to be envious. Books (i.e., of poetry) have been filled with the censure of envy, and every man of intelligence knows how much has been said as to its baseness. It is necessary to turn from it, for frequently the affairs of the envious lead him to use violence. Thus it is said of such as these, "And they covet fields and take them by violence." Enviousness is a loathsome trait. The wise man must keep himself as far from it as he can, for he gains no advantage through it: on the contrary, continued depression and fatigue of the spirit through desires and the constant hatred of men, scantiness of repose, preoccupation of the mind, apprehensiveness and the punishment of God, for transgressing that which He forbade in His revealed Scripture. Man must not be jealous of unrighteous men, because he sees them devote themselves to pleasure and (the gratifying of) passions. But let him employ his zeal in the service of God. Thus the sage said, "Let not thy heart be envious of the sinners." Again, he spake, "Be thou not envious against the workers of iniquity."

Zeal is goodly only in the service of God, as thou knowest from (the case of) Phinehas, of whom it is said, "While he was zealous for my sake," and the good reward which he merited thereby, as it is said, "Wherefore, say, behold I give unto him my covenant of peace."

Among the things which have been said with reference to the jealous and envious (we find), "Thou wilt observe the envious man effusive in his affection (for thee) when he meets thee, but hating thee in thy absence. His name is friend, his intention unfriendly." Again it has been said, "It appears as though the envious were created in order to be angered." Furthermore it has been said, "Let it suffice for thee that the envious man is grieved at the time of thy joy." It is incumbent upon man to mount to such an exalted rank with the aid of his powers and gifts, that he be envied therefor. Let him ponder over this, as saith the poet: "Lo, I was envied, but God increased men's enviousness touching me. Let man rather not live at all than live for a single day unenvied. Man is not envied save for his excellences, which are forbearance, scholarship, nobility, and generosity."

Chapter 4

TREATING OF WIDE-AWAKEDNESS

I Must preface, in treating of this quality, of what nature it is derived. I would hold that it is of the yellow-gall species. This quality appears usually when the soul is free from other blamable qualities and when it is not mingled with aught of grief, and most frequently it is (found) in pure and noble souls. It is a commendable quality, and man ought to make use of it in whatsoever work of art or science he be engrossed. Was it not said of him, "The substance of a wide-awake man is precious," which means that the most precious virtue of the lofty is wide-awakedness, both in the present and future life. In the world de generation et corruption, he is wide-awake in his quest of knowledge as well as goodness of service and faith, and in the attempt to attain to the world of intellect.

With reference to the reverse of this quality, that is, weakness of purpose in worldly affairs and in the attempt to save souls, it has been said, "If thou faint in the day of adversity thy strength is small"; and again, "The slothful man roasteth not that which he took in hunting." However, we have mentioned the languid while treating of the quality of hatred. He who is one of the estimable, and administers his affairs with alacrity, will succeed in them. Thus it is said, "The hand of the diligent shall bear rule; but the slothful shall be under tribute." Concerning this the poet spake: "If the souls become too greatly ambitious, the bodies will be wearied thereby." This is a beautiful maxim. The sage, peace be upon him, exhorted to wide-awakedness in matters religious and worldly in saying, "Slothfulness casteth into a deep sleep." This saying is very evident, for slothfulness necessarily induces lethargy. For when the vapors, which are designed to exude from the pores of the body through forcible movements, are motionless and do not dissolve, they mount to the brain, and bring about constant drowsiness. In the book of Al-Kuti it is said of wide-awakedness, "He who satisfies his land in respect of cultivation, will be satisfied by it with bread."

The ethical aspect of this quality is, "Man must not display it in his lust." He shall not be rash through this in his wrath, for rashness is blameworthy since it is not one of the qualities of the wise. The excellent do not make use of it. But one ought to employ wide-awakedness in matters relating to religion and law. The surest reason for the success of a man is (to be found in) the wide-awakedness with which he conducts his affairs, and the greatest sign of misfortune is his slothfulness with regard to them. The poet has said: "The pure and noble souls are wakeful, watchful, and sound of judgment, while the stupid and heavy souls are drowsy, mean, and low." But that intense wide-awakedness which leads to hastiness is culpable. Let the intelligent man beware of using it, for it is the very worst of evils. He who is hasty, rushes to destruction, and the man of hastiness is not secure from disappointment. A verse reads: "A cautious man will realize his desires. But he who hastens unduly is bound to stumble." Man must not make undue haste in his affairs, because no good result can be obtained by haste, but through deliberation ends are (more) easily attained. The beauty of the state of wide-awakedness lies in its being potential in the soul and not appearing quickly in action.

Chapter 1

TREATING OF THE QUALITY OF LIBERALITY (GENEROSITY)

This quality, when it is employed with moderation and does not lapse into prodigality, is commendable. Man must prefer this quality to its antithesis, for example, the quality of niggardliness, since the great men who are renowned by reason of their excellences are not convinced that niggardliness is a praise-worthy quality.

Dost thou not see, may God guide thee aright, in how many places the sage extols the man who is generous? In one place he says that liberality brings a man to many degrees of eminence in this world and in the world to come. Thus, it is said, "A man's gift maketh room for him and bringeth him before great men" in this world, because it brings him near to kings whose good-will he gain through gifts; as thou knowest from the respect of Ben Hadad for Asa, and Tiglath for Ahaz, because presents were made to them,

And in the world to come he will attain the merited (share of its) bliss, which man realizes because of his serving the Lord with his substance in almsgiving. Thus it is said, "Therefore will I divide him a portion with the great." Since liberality was a virtue of our father Abraham, peace be upon him, he became known thereby and it was ascribed to him. This quality is attributed to him in the Holy Scripture in several places, and thus is to be understood the explanation of, "The generous of the people are gathered together, even the people of the God of Abraham." This is a commendable quality because it secures honor for him who exercises it. Thus, it is said (P, "Many will entreat the favor of the generous, and every man is a friend to him that giveth gifts."

Through this a man merits his fellow-men's praise when he gives generously, and he is lauded therefor. Thus spake a poet: "When thou goest to him, thou wilt find him of pleasant demeanor as if thou wert about to give him what he will give thee. Had he naught but his life to give, he would give this. Wherefore, let the fear of God be upon whomsoever would ask this of him." But the unseemly side of this quality appears when man wastes his substance needlessly and mismanages it; as, for instance, he who spends it in devotion to pleasures and in gratifying his lust. This is squandering and is not characteristic of the wise.

A gift in the right place is a treasure put aside. It perisheth not in the course of time, but abideth with the ages. This is the opinion of Solomon, peace be upon him, who said, "Cast thy bread upon the waters; for thou shalt find it after many days." This verse evidently exhorts to generosity, for if man be generous and bountiful, he will reap the fruit thereof. Thus spake the poet: "Sow thou generosity in the field of gifts, and noble deeds shall be harvested by thee early." Wherefore man ought to know that if he be in a prosperous condition, then his generosity will not impair his prosperity, and if he be in a straitened condition, his adversity will not continue on that account. It is peculiar to this noble quality, that he who employs it never feels the want of anything; on the contrary, his abundance is much increased. Thus it is said: "He that giveth unto the poor shall not lack." Furthermore, David the Saint, peace be upon him, says of generous and liberal men, "He hath dispersed, he hath given to the poor: his righteousness endureth forever." What is your opinion with reference to the use of this gracious virtue? It is like lending unto God, exalted and magnified is He. Thus the saying, "He that hath pity upon the poor lendeth unto the Lord." Thus it was said in the book on Ethics: "Bestow kindness on those who are worthy and upon those who are unworthy. In the case of the worthy, thy kindness will be in the right place; and in the case of the unworthy, prove thou thy worth." Again, it was said with reference to liberality, "It is a part of the noble qualities to give liberally to him who asks."

In the book of Al-Kuti (it is said): "Know thou that resolution consists in doing things with firmness. Consider well when to yield and when to deny, when to grant and when to promise. For a gift after denying is better than denying after (promising) a gift and favor. Setting out to do after consideration is better than to abandon after setting out. Know that thou shouldst be more prompt to do what thou hast not promised, than to promise what thou wilt not do. Therefore, beware of hastily promising what thou fearest thou mayest be unable to perform. Adorn thy promise with truth and thy deed with justice."

Chapter 2

TREATING OF NIGGARDLINESS

Know thou that this is a reprehensible quality. Among the host of reprehensible qualities there is none more abominable than this. For thou seest that he who is lavishly bountiful of his substance, although blameworthy, is satisfied with the pleasure he derives and men's goodly praise which is his. But niggardliness is accompanied by evil repute without even the attainment of pleasure; and to be of evil repute is not one of the qualities desired by the excellent. The noble-minded man ought to shrink from this quality and not employ it on any occasion. The sages are at one in thinking that manliness does not go well with prodigality, nor religion with an inordinate desire (for gain). He who is of this character may well despair of a good repute and a fair record. Thus, it was said, "The vile person shall be no more called liberal, nor the churl said to be bountiful." This "vile person" is like him, in the wilderness of Maon, who said, "Shall I then take my bread and my water...and give it unto men whom I know not whence they be?" Thou knowest the severe punishment with which he met.

But the good feature of this state is that man does not squander his substance, be it great or small, but guards it by means of this quality. He must not overdo this, however, lest he pass over to the quality of greed, which is not of the qualities of the noble. Thus, the sage spake in condemning niggardliness, "He that withholdeth corn, the people shall curse him"; and, on the contrary,

"Blessing shall be on the head of him that selleth it." This verse outwardly refers to "charity," but its hidden implication is knowledge. The wise man ought not be niggardly in dealing out his knowledge, for knowledge is not lessened by imparting it (to others), as little as the brightness of the fire dies away when a light is kindled therefrom. The best rule with regard to the employment of this quality is to accustom one's self to beneficence toward kinsmen, until one gradually habituate one's self to benevolence toward strangers, and thus train one's self to choose generosity.

Chapter 3

TREATING OF VALOR

The man who prevails over the temperament of the blood-nature, who is large-hearted, full-veined, and long-armed, thou wilt generally find to be a man of valor, especially if, combined with that, he be master of the art of war. This quality is praiseworthy (in man), when it is manifested in his strength, and in accordance with his determination to be saved from what might befall him. But when he departs from a moderate course and unites valor with the quality of folly and it becomes the cause of a man's throwing himself into dangerous places then it is reprehensible.

Of these two dispositions the sage saith, "Happy is the man that feareth always; but he that hardeneth his heart shall fall into mischief." But as regards the great men who are mentioned as possessors of this quality, heavenly signs gave evidence of their possessing this power, thus Joshua, Gideon, Samson, Saul, David, Jonathan, Joab, and Abner, and others like them, whose power gave evidence of the quality of valor, were praised therefor; and those whose weakness, in contradistinction to the former, gave evidence of the quality of cowardice, were not commended for it, as I will show in regard to them in the following chapter.

It is necessary to devote this quality to the service of God, as thou knowest from (the story of) Moses, peace be upon him, when he retaliated upon the people by saying to the children of Levi, "Put every man his sword by his side"; and as thou knowest from Phinehas in the matter of his zeal. Thus it is said, "And when Phinehas, the son of Aaron the priest, saw it, he rose up from among the congregation and took a javelin in his hand." This quality of valor never fails to be conspicuous in the souls of mighty men and courageous heroes. With reference to valor and patience in facing danger, the poet spake: "There came a day in the heat of which some people warmed themselves, but though there was no fire, they acted as if in the fire's midst. But we had patience until the day was done. Likewise, a case of misfortune can be brought to a close only through patience." Among the things which have been said in order to encourage the use of valor is: "Crave death, and life will be granted thee." The Arabs were accustomed to call the man of valor "safe."

Among the things which have been said on the emboldening of the spirit in combat is the word of the poet: "I went to the rear to preserve my life (in battle), but I found that I could not preserve my life unless I went forward." Thus, the noble man must make use of this quality in such a way as not to overstep the middle path lest he be called demented (foolhardy). But he must pursue an excellent course in regard to this quality. The philosopher spake, "The extreme limit of valor is strength and endurance with respect to what thou abhorrest." Valor cannot go hand-in-hand with vanity (untruth), nor firmness with absurdity, nor patience with weariness, for these are of the qualities of asses and swine. Valor consists in persevering in the right and overcoming thy desires, until thou feel that to die in the best way, thou hast found is more desirable than to live in the opposite For example (evil) way, which the power of understanding may have revealed to thee. According to Al-Kuti, "Valor is the nature of a noble soul, corresponding to the strength of the body."

Chapter 4

TREATING OF COWARDICE

This quality is generally found in spirits that are abject and downcast, poor and wretched. It is a reprehensible quality. Let the wise man be on his guard against it, let him make no use of it, exert himself to keep away and abstain from it, since he derives no benefit from it; on the contrary, he reaps ill repute, a vile record, and a diminution of praise. Men of lofty purpose must dread it when they have learned to employ their power of distinguishing in the use of things, so that it may be the means of escaping serious danger.

Among the offshoots of this quality is slothfulness, of which we have already treated. Thou knowest what was said with regard to its ignominy and baseness. Thus the sage, peace be upon him, said, "A slothful man hideth his hand in his bosom, and will not so much as bring it to his mouth again." This is the uttermost that can be said of the shame thereof. The slothful coward is known to say: "I will not travel, for fear of highwaymen and wild beasts. I will not engage in business, lest I meet with losses. I will not fast, lest I become ill. I will give no alms, lest I become poor," and similar words that put an end to all activity, until there remains nothing for him to do, but living on without moving from his place, as it is said ("As the door turneth upon its hinges, so doth the slothful upon his bed." A wise man should not choose this quality of cowardice or make use thereof in preference to his other qualities, lest he become known thereby.

And be as one who fancies that he will be killed before the expiration of the appointed time, as was said exaggeratedly of the slothful coward by the poet, who spake thus: "If a little bird merely raises its voice, the heart of the coward is consumed (leaps with terror). But his teeth are sharp as iron, at meal times." But in a case where escape is impossible, it is permissible for the quality of cowardice to come into play as in the case of him, concerning whom it is said: "The king dispatched him to a dangerous place. He refused to go. The king reviled him, whereupon he said, 'It is better that thou revile me when living than bless me when dead.'" It has been said that this quality has been made use of by those who prefer repose in this world to all other qualities, not knowing that repose can be enjoyed to the full, only after zealous care in the regulating of affairs and the attainment of whatsoever be needed. Thus, it is said, "Prepare thy work without, and make it fit for thyself in the field." Repose in and of itself signifies slothfulness and cowardice.

Thou knowest what happens to a man by reason of his slothfulness: namely, he is deprived of all his honor through utter poverty. Thus, it is said: "Yet a little sleep, a little slumber, a little folding of the hands to sleep: so, shall thy poverty come as one that travelleth, and thy want as an armed man." Again, this quality engenders in the body not a few ills and diseases, thus flabbiness, dullness, swelling, gout, sciatica, and elephantiasis, and similarly whatsoever results from indigestion; in fact, this quality becomes habitual to a man and he considers everything else as faulty and worthless; especially if this feeble coward be of a phlegmatic disposition and on the way to old age, then it weighs him down even more.

Thus, thou hast, May God have mercy upon thee, all that was promised in the introduction. Because of our love of conciseness, our aversion to prolixity, and our fear of departing from the purpose of the book, we have much curtailed the discourse in the individual chapters and in the various parts. We have not united every one of these qualities to its nature and its sense, nor have we referred the senses to their natures, although we ought to make clear the situation of every quality in the body and give much of the science of the temperaments, anatomy and physiognomy. We think, however, that this must be deferred to some other time, when it may please God, exalted may He be, for He is the One from whom to seek help. Having finished as much as we could, and having said enough in the chapters of this book, we would hold it to be possible that there exist in man qualities other than those which have been classified, and still other natures. We say yes. We have been brief with regard to the others for two reasons: First, we know that among the qualities of men are those of vexation and weariness.

We feared that these might occupy as much space as the whole book, and therefore we did not go to the length of collecting many verses from the Hebrew and Arabic. Furthermore, because we knew that there is no quality which we have avoided mentioning, that is not implied among those which have been mentioned. It would bear the same relation to them that the branches do to the root. If anyone should happen to say, "Thou must not exhort men to improve their qualities, nor arouse them concerning the betterment of their moral status, unless this be characteristic of thine own self because thou wouldst be as he who recommends piety and forgets himself" we would reply, "Every vessel gives forth whatever it contains." How foolish is he who seeks to measure this world and does not know the value of the Parasang wherewith it is measured. We have not mentioned any excellence which we have not emulated; nor have we extolled any quality which we have not tried to make part of our own nature. He who adorns himself with what is not in him, will find his claims laid bare after a time.

To Him that giveth understanding do I owe thanks: with Him do I triumph: in Him do I greatly glory: with Him do I take refuge against such things (as those aforementioned). Him do I praise for he is worthy of praise; to Him it belongs and Him praise behooves. Thus spake His saint, peace be upon him, "I will greatly praise the Lord with my mouth; yes, I will praise Him among the multitude. For He shall stand at the right hand of the poor to save him from those that condemn his soul." Thus is ended what I sought to establish in the book on "The Improvement of the Qualities," with the help of God and His assistance. He is my lot and my fortune, the Helper and the Giver of aid. Praise be to God, the Lord of both worlds! Blessed be the Merciful who hath helped us!